TO BE NAMED SOMETHING ELSE

Miller Williams Poetry Series
EDITED BY PATRICIA SMITH

TO BE NAMED SOMETHING ELSE

◆ ◆ ◆

Shaina Phenix

The University of Arkansas Press
Fayetteville
2023

ISBN: 978-1-68226-228-3
eISBN: 978-1-61075-793-5

27 26 25 24 23   5 4 3 2 1

Manufactured in the United States of America

Designed by Liz Lester
Cover image: The author pictured as an infant with her grandmother in Harlem, 1995
Cover design: Anthony Blake

♾ The paper used in this publication meets the minimum requirements of the American National Standard for Permanence of Paper for Printed Library Materials Z39.48-1984.

Library of Congress Cataloging-in-Publication Data

Names: Phenix, Shaina, author.
Title: To be named something else / Shaina Phenix.
Description: Fayetteville: The University of Arkansas Press, 2023. | Series: Miller
   Williams poetry series | Summary: "To Be Named Something Else, winner of the
   2023 Miller Williams Poetry Prize, is a high-spirited celebration of Black matriar-
   chy and lineage—both familial and literary. Centering the coming-of-age of Black
   femmes in Harlem, Shaina Phenix's debut collection, in the words of series judge
   Patricia Smith, 'enlivens the everyday—the everyday miraculous, the everyday
   hallelujah, the numbing everyday love, the everyday risk of just being Black and
   living.'"—Provided by publisher.
Identifiers: LCCN 2022050614 (print) | LCCN 2022050615 (ebook) |
   ISBN 9781682262283 (paperback; alk. paper) | ISBN 9781610757935 (ebook)
Subjects: LCGFT: Poetry.
Classification: LCC PS3616.H4464 T6 2023 (print) | LCC PS3616.H4464
   (ebook) | DDC 811/.6—dc23/eng/20221021
LC record available at https://lccn.loc.gov/2022050614
LC ebook record available at https://lccn.loc.gov/2022050615

Supported by the Miller and Lucinda Williams Poetry Fund

for Kendi, Bailee, & every Black girl
for my mother, for her mother

CONTENTS

So you'd think, in the second year of my three-year term as Miller Williams Poetry Prize series editor, that I've clicked into a rhythm, undaunted by the hundreds of spectacular submissions flooding my inbox, and reliant on my stellar crew of screeners—all schooled in my exacting standards—to sift through all the goodness and present me with fifty stunners, from which I pluck the three clear winners, each one having risen to the top of the pile with the relentlessness of a north star.

Whew. *That* is overwritten.

But really—I'm not sure how folks picture this task, but it is, in turns, mystifying, exhilarating, and utterly impossible.

At the very heart of the difficulty is that age-old question, *What makes a good poem?* I have been confronted with that pesky query hundreds of times—served up by grade-schoolers, bookstore patrons, confounded undergrads, reading groups, festivalgoers, workshop participants, curious onlookers, byliners and bystanders, and folks just looking to make conversation when I tell them what I do. (And no—it's not just you—it took a *long* time before I was able to state "I am a poet" without tacking on something that felt legitimizing and more jobby, like ". . . oh, and a greeter at Walmart.")

What makes a good poem depends very much on who's doing the reading, when they're doing the reading, and issues and insight they brought to the table before starting to read. It's insanely subjective. At the beginning of my appointment as series editor (I almost said "at the beginning of my reign"—must be the scepter Billy Collins passed down to me), I was asked what kind of poems constituted the books I'd be looking for. Here's what I said:

> I love poems that vivify and disturb. No matter what genre we write in, we're all essentially storytellers—but it's poets who toil most industriously, telling huge unwieldy stories within tight and gorgeously controlled confines, stories that are structurally and sonically adventurous, and it's magic every time it happens. Simply put, when I read a poetry book, I want something to shift in my chest. I want my world to change.

That obviously was one bridge too far for a few folks, who wailed on social media—the primary forum for wailing—that my standards were merely unattainable. One incensed Tweeter (or is it "Tweeterer"?) was particularly riled by the "shift in my chest / world change" thing.

Who in their right mind believes that poetry can actually change the world? THIS world? Why are we teaching our younguns such lofty dribble? Why should the average poet submit a manuscript with absolutely no chance of shifting anything in this strange woman's chest? Alas, come down from that mountain, Madam Editor—can mere mortals get a break?

I want to repeat—and clarify—that good poetry should not leave you the same as when you came to it. I see that as a relatively simple ask on the part of the poet:

> *I have a story. It's a familiar story, but I'm going to tell it in a way you haven't heard before. I want to give the story to you. Take it with you. Live it.*
> *Now my story is part of your story.*

You'd be amazed at how many things I've felt that way about. The way Boo screeches "Kitty!" at the end of the film *Monsters, Inc.* A hard-rhymed scrawl by a sixth grader at Lillie C. Evans Elementary School in the Liberty City section of Miami. A poem written by a student of mine at Princeton—structured like an application form, it morphed into a heartbreaking and revealing piece about his being embarrassed by his aging mother. The children's book *Don't Let the Pigeon Ride the Bus!*. Everything ever penned by Gwendolyn Brooks. The one and only poem written by a reticent mumbler in my Staten Island Intro to Creative Writing class, because it was his one and only poem and he said he'd never write a poem at all. "Antarctica Considers Her Explorers" by Diane Ackerman. The song "Ooo Baby Baby" as crooned by one Smokey Robinson.

I say all that to say this: I am moved by many things, none of them perfection. None of them haughty or precise or manipulative. None of them professional or studied or "officially sanctioned" in any way. I seldom know what I need until it has arrived. I do know that that shift in my chest, that rock to my world, can come from anywhere—somewhere simple, somewhere complex. Anywhere a moment, a voice, a song, or a poem reaches out and finds someone.

I can assure you that the three winners of this year's Miller Williams series are all—I've checked—mere mortals. Each one took a different road to reach me; each one changed my world in a different way. There is no one voice, and there is no one way to hear a voice.

Let's look at the winners, from third to first, from runners-up to crown, Miss America style.

Red Ocher by Jessica Poli is a lush collision of aubade, cento and ghazal, poems that snug cozily into forms that were born waiting for them, poems that pulse outward from a relentless core of sensuality and heartbreak to embody what nature does to us. I am wholly envious of Jessica, because I find such concise lyricism to be difficult to manage. And having grown up surrounded by concrete and hard edges where pigeons were the only wildlife, I can't help but be mesmerized by a poem like "The Morning After"—

> When I opened the door to the coop
> and saw three chickens and a mallard lying dead

in the soggy pine chips, I thought the raccoon
had made clean kills of all the birds it wanted

in the night. So forgive me if I shouted
when I walked into the yard and saw the duck

standing motionless, head covered in blood,
a marble statue after a war.

What's stamped on me, what follows me into my dreaming, is the instance after, the necessary sacrifice of the dying duck, who flees, headless, "before it stopped / and sank to the ground where its neck arced / and swung, mourning itself."

What I'm changed by is the breath I hold in from the beginning of the title poem "Red Ocher":

To paint the barn bloody.

After all that planting, the peppers rot off the vine.

Wind was once oil. Soil has memories.

What's lost in the retelling.

To fall apart or believe.

The farmer, filling the wheelbarrow with sawdust, remembering last year's
weather: *That was a different God.*

What the wasp dragging its half-severed tail knows about sorrow.

Jessica teaches a softer violence, the tender face of it. Her deftly crafted stanzas, her mastery of form, her lean uncluttered way of nudging us forward—all those things make *Red Ocher* a book that undeniably deserves the accolades coming its way.

Up next—well hello there, Ms. L. J. Sysko! You are a wildness and a weirdness, and I would like to play a role in unleashing you upon the world. Your book, *The Daughter of Man*, is gleeful and quicksilver, not willing to sit still for categorization. I'm *here* for it.

L. J. is the risk-taker, the unveiler, the irreverent namer of things. Witness "Trompe L'Oeil," a disrespectful ode to a former teacher:

Like a kid climbing through the window: eyes wide, shirt billowing
open with the heat of hijinks, I'm back—grabbing you by the Peter
Pan collar to chew gum in your class, drop your hall pass in the toilet,
and eat your breakfast for lunch. I won't recover my manners, no,
they're pinned up there under the postcards, ribboned fast to a bulletin

board between lion and lamb. You sat the girls in the back of the class and taught math to the front. And I guess I have the option of being less mad, but my upset's been tipping on the precipice forever, like a Medici cherub poised for a rotunda-fall.

Let's take a wee tour of L. J.'s mind, shall we? Up next, from the poem "I may":

> If I want, I may ultrasound each month to monitor
> hornets' nest activity. I may bushwhack to witness
> watering-hole power dynamics. If I want, I may
> write ethnographies about cultural reciprocity
> or muse at the wisdom of using blood as currency.
> It's my vagina/uterus/cervix, so you can't tell me
> I haven't wasted whole days microscope-hunched,
> waiting for something to happen.
> Days wishing happenings would stop.

Who can stop there? See more of what I saw:

What's stupid

is, even if aliens do
mean us harm and descend
the way they did in comic books—
all jumbo-almond eyes, peach-pit heads,
and pistachio-ice-cream skin,
knocking the totem off Bob's Big Boy roof,
even if they utter language that's frozen and vegetable,
even if, with weapons drawn or peace in our puny hearts,
we're vaporized, liquefied, or harvested as fuel—I'll still feel
the jubilant force of epiphany. The way a pearl peering out
of a knife-pried oyster might behold a kitchen.
The way a woman dwelling within a paneled parlor
might put the phone receiver down,
return to preparing dinner, folding laundry,
Gunsmoke or *Green Acres*,
having just heard
the unutterable word.

The Daughter of Man is gleefully unapologetic, upending the familiar and blasting it with motion, heat, and consequence. It's a wide-eyed stroll through the real world, reintroducing me to moments I just might remember living—moments made new with liberal dashes of L. J.'s humor and singular insight.

This year's Miller Williams Poetry Prize top choice, *To Be Named Something Else* by Shaina Phenix, absolutely refuses to behave on the page. Something shifted in my chest with the book's very first poem, because I know—actually, was one of—those blue-black summer girls waiting for some bad boys to twist open the fire hydrant and cool us off:

> See us,   summered in waters most definitely troubled,   stubborn & never
> actually putting any fires out,   rinsing our summertime heavies down into
>   the sewers.
> Little Black   so & so's   walk through water   like we Moses or something.
> See her, all copper & running over   like she God, a cup,   or something.

With "Hydrant Ode," and with so many of the other poems that make up this electric collection, Shaina enlivens the everyday—the everyday miraculous, the everyday hallelujah, the numbing everyday love, the everyday risk of just being Black and living.

There is absolutely nowhere these poems aren't—we're dancing and sweating through our clothes, terminating a pregnancy in a chilled room of white and silver, finally gettin' those brows threaded and nails did, practicing gettin' the Holy Ghost, sending folks to their rest, having babies, listening carefully to the lessons of elders, and sometimes even talking back.

In the brilliant "La Femme Noire: A Choreopoem," a piece in conversation with Ntozake Shange's *For Colored Girls Who Have Considered Suicide / When the Rainbow Is Enuf*, a young Black girl ("perhaps myself," Shaina suggests) queries the elders in an attempt to pull them closer:

> *Who are you and whom do you love?*
>
> *What do you remember about blood?*
>
> *Who is responsible for the suffering of your mother?*
>
> *Tell me something you've never said to your body.*

Of course, I did what all the fortunate readers of this book will inevitably do. I walked into the poem and answered every question for myself. And with my answers, I found new pathways, new ways to be drawn into Shaina's work.

To Be Named Something Else is a book of reason and reckoning, substance and shadow. It's tender and wide-aloud and just about everything we need right now, when both reason and reckoning are in such woefully short supply. And Shaina's superlative combination of formalism and funk consistently astounds—deftly crafted ghazals, sonnets, the pantoum, the duplex, the sestina, and other usta-be traditional structures (I say "usta-be" because they are hereafter transformed) are all on display here.

And not simply on display. They come to conquer.

Every page is stamped with a defiant signature—in fact, I guarantee there's no way you can flip past "Shug Avery Identifies as Pansexual, Poly, and Dares You to Say Anything about It," "The Burning Haibun Remembers Who I Am," or "American Pantoum with Bullet-Holes & Wall." Shaina Phenix will pull in you, and she will hold you there. And, by God, you won't want to move.

I leave you with a stanza from "Sermon," one that resounds with me, if any one stanza can be said to typify the power of this collection:

> Mother god in the name of Girl—I come to you
> as alive as I know how asking you to be
> an unbloodied knuckle sandwich, be unfucked, and in
> an undulant ocean of selves and salt bone of my befores. Be the first word
> out of my mother's reborn mouth. Be swine-repellent or the pearls that look
> like pearls but don't bust from too much pressing   down. Be that
> which is holy and make dogs deathly allergic. Be
> me in an un-rendable skin-sheet. Let this poem (Earth? Body?) ? Be all of you
> and none of me for the sake of your people.   Amen.

—*Patricia Smith*

TO BE NAMED SOMETHING ELSE

The poet Sonia Sanchez, who taught "The Bluest Eye" in her classroom at Temple University, saw the book as an indictment of American culture . . . Sanchez told me, "For this woman, Toni Morrison, to write this, to show this to us—it was the possible death of a people right there, the death of a younger generation that had been so abused that there was really no hope. What Toni has done with her literature is that she has made us look up and see ourselves. She has authenticated us, and she has also said to America, in a sense, 'Do you know what you did? But, in spite of what you did, here we is. We exist. Look at us.'"

—Hilton Als, from "Toni Morrison and the Ghosts in the House"

She been tryna get seen without getting got. Wants to be remembered, for more than the ripped stitch of her first name—thick with acrylic clicks of her momma's first honest prayer ever written in ink.

—Faylita Hicks, from the poem
"About the Girl Who Would Become a Gawd"

if i am ever less than a mountain
for your definite brothers and sisters
let the rivers pour over my head
let the sea take me for a spiller

—Lucille Clifton, from "the lost baby poem"

HYDRANT ODE

Wade in the water, wade in the water, children

See that girl all dressed in red   her rust, her accumulation of trashed things gathered
around her like a garden? Her three parts rivering   against sun-slicked Harlem
kids whose giggles make waves in her wet.   Ever met a so & so's daddy romancing
her with a sweat-piled tank top & a wrench? Asking her to watch his kids

while he go down the block, play his numbers?   Sometimes she hard to get,
trickle a little,   & send so & so's daddy on his way,   water-poor.   & sometimes
she get full off the weeping of a hoodsummer's   souls caught & bodies graved,
get full off somebody mama scrubbing blood stain,   off somebody best friend

since shawties with lit candles at the corner vigil   & she burst
boutade, billow, bayou, on the curb. See Black   & water sparkled
young painted in floral neoprene, supermarket plastic caps,   icee red, green, or blue
lips crescent,   & flip-flops making beats against a parched asphalt getting quenched.

She done seen a Black child or two   alive & right before her eyes,   done doused
them in her blessed faucet spit,   done sapped the blood from scraped
knees, done washed the face of a wandering   toddler hollering cause they dropped
their ice cream cone   in the street,   done been a block-side carwash,   sink

to clean the grill after cookout,   been meeting spot for heat-wave kisses,   been pool when
pool gets closed cause twelve like us better with nothing to do,   been an
ocean we brought our own salt to: oil-drenched pastelitos, chicken spot hot wings, Jimbos
fries, Taste of Seafood fish sandwiches, Funyuns, sunflower seeds.

See us,   summered in waters most definitely troubled,   stubborn & never
actually putting any fires out,   rinsing our summertime heavies down into the sewers.
Little Black   so & so's   walk through water   like we Moses or something.
See her, all copper & running over   like she God, a cup,   or something.

3

GIRL – ROOT

LUCILLE

if i be you
at all, let me not forget
to celebrate between starshine and clay
and every day   something
has tried against my mouth
you built   against the making
hands mold in your image
and failed and failed
and Dorothy
if i be yours
one day, let me not forget
the skin of summer spent well,
forest curls at the kitchen table
smelling of your blood and
never calling you   grandmother
or you—you
still smelling blood
saying *gran* and praying
the day
believing God for its inevitability
and Shirldina
if i be you
in the body, let me not forget
the swell of your ocean
into a language
you call jada, i
call mother
lending your blood
to four babies
with mountain mouths
stitched in a legion
of things misplaced and found.
and Bettie

if i be yours
one day, let me not forget
the mirror you made of everything
but your blood, the look
into me, never watching
for spread of nose, never
for something i could not be
if i tried.

THE BURNING HAIBUN REMEMBERS WHO I AM

Somewhere I got the idea that my love is an Xbox controller. My love is a hardened & thick gobbet of nonrecyclable material to be clicked at & jiggered in a web of sweat-wet fingers. My love is to be tossed in a floor's face, a thing to eventually break. My love is the too-long accomplice of lovers with their asses pinned to couch or carpet when we cannot afford a couch, gunning down the simulated masses of folks on a perhaps-street of a very real city somewhere in the name of a god, a complex that took root in their bellies after something already dead suggested pretend homicides could dim their unavoidable black ache. My love is something that should take what it gets. Get filled & emptied at the whim of bodies with breath in them. My love *kee-kees* when I mean to ask, *do you have any idea who the fuck you're dealing with?* I am Roma Jean's great-granddaughter, who up until she battled her bones into an earth, was   the game, was game, was player, an anatomy of w's. Roma Jean was a penny slot rigged to jackpot every time a mothafucka pulled the right lever. Roma Jean was a jackpot—with lovers who knew nothing but worship at the gold coins of her feet, at the groves in her high-payout thighs. Somewhere I was convinced that I lacked her ofness because my love had been a recurring & boiled over jackpot emptied into worship-thin hands, brobdingnagian bodies of potential. Somewhere, I called my love lack & stayed where I should have at least metaphorically hoisted every piece of ended love's clothing over a balcony. Somewhere, I should have let Roma Jean's gold-blood spill a little on the letter I'd write to say, *Dear love, you really screwed this one up & I am no game to play in the way that there are no do-overs here, you can't pay your way back into living, here & there is no love like mine, but I wish you something close, a life of semblance.* By blood, I too am a recrudescing body of win. By blood, I too am jackpot-boned. In the earth under me now, is ofness— my grandmother Shirl, my great-grandmother Roma Jean, my great-great-grandmother Sarah—all clanging like gold bricks & hootin & hollerin bout everything my love is.

//

Somewhere   my love is hardened   nonrecyclable &   sweat-wet   My love is a floor   , a   break accomplice of lovers we cannot afford perhaps-street of a very real city somewhere

in the name of a God,   a   root
something already

black   .   my love
get filled &   at the whim of   breath
. My love *kee-kees*   asks, *do you have any idea*
who the fuck you're dealing with? I am Roma Jean's
great-granddaughter,
the game,   player,   anatomy of w's.
a penny slot rigged to jackpot every time
the right lever.   with
lovers who know nothing but worship   gold coins of   feet,
the groves in   high-payout thighs. Somewhere I was
        her ofness   my love   a recurring &
boiled over jackpot emptied into worship
brobdingnagian bodies of

gold-blood spill   I
say, *Dear love, you*
            are   *here,*
        living here & there is no love like mine,   *I wish you*
                        blood   too,   a
recrudescing body of win.   too,   jackpot-boned
        love is   win. In the earth   is
ofness—   Shirl,   Roma Jean,
        Sarah—all clanging like gold bricks
    &   my love is

//

I got the idea
My love is   a sweat-wet   God
is   a   gold-   spill earth

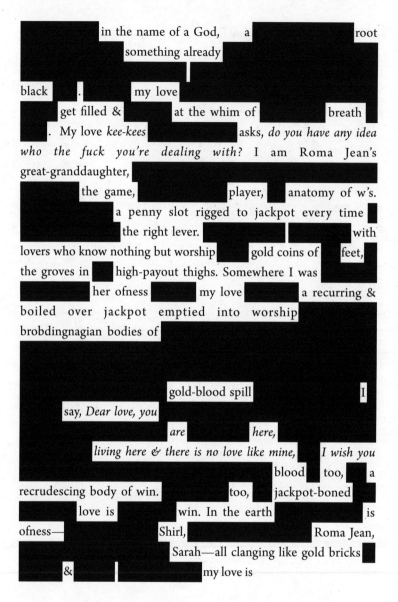
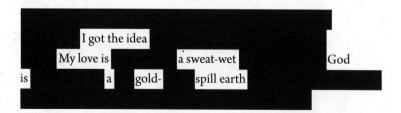

10

NONG

"If they used it against you, it is yours to make sing."

—Franny Choi

What is that sound in your mouth?
Nigger bones found quartered in a creek:
And what is all this fussin about?

Jiganinny-jiganinny jeze-mammy ne - gress nigg-er nigg-er bi - tchtch
A hymnal of bosom, budding black babes, baring all things in her back. Hear her song—does it weep?
What is that sound in her mouth?

This: A *Neegar*, the *Negar*, and my *Niggor* praise their feet into a holy floor when they shout.
NiggaGod got bronze and deep skin and sheep hair. NiggaGod assembles his blood into brun batik.
And what is all this   fussin about?

Negro   buck, Nig-child   buckwheat, Brute   get beat   down south
The toast-burnt collarbones and sun-soaked scapulas scat   to their graves and the black-boned
     earth creaks.
What is the sound   mouth?

El mayate, tar baby, little sambo lose   their fingers in each other's scalps.
And the blooded and nubbed hands   play djembe for all young and black fingerless   peace.
And what is all that fussin   about?

La la la negra, la la la nigga, la la la commodious and gorgeous mouths,
Oh what a lovely precious dream, to be Black, *soul*   *intact*, singing   the blood-black songs.
And what   is all this ~~fussin~~ about?
What sound is in your mouth?

CENTO

Since I thought I'd be dead by now everything I do is fucking perfect.

Listen to me. I am telling you a true thing. This is the only kingdom.

A name wedged between an organ's teeth, a name   pumping

in my gut, awakened by the more I'd wanted: to taste

I have only to break into the tightness of a strawberry, and I see summer.

I have walked by the memory of others   between the blood night   and twilights.

I knew I had it. What my mother and my mother's mother before her had.

I am a Black woman   stripped down and praying   my whole life has been an altar.

What did I know about waters rushing back   what did I know about drowning?

Where did it start? In a city of gardens and muck.

On the brick red stoop of the brownstone next door.

And a sweet daughter mingled with the dead.

The smell of all oceans was around us—steamy salt, shell, and sweat

hearing the beat of unsung poems in every voice,   visiting the haunted rooms in every face.

This time, this poem, is the best idea I've ever had—the best in history even

and I ran after it like prey, as if I knew it had to be mine. I salivated

as tambourines hitting cornbread hips black

and glorious   dripping droplets   orbs of holy   water.

There are many ways to look at this.

A sunflower somehow planted   in the alley. Its broken neck.

My mother's name. The name I had, too, for the first part of my life,

a good name, borrowed from the sky

of wild behavior, indiscriminate coloring, and only

some day, when trees have shed their leaves

I can turn toward you, whoever you are, and say you are my lover simply because everything want to be loved.

I am yet to learn the difference between pleasure and fear

and there are millions of leaves collecting against the curbs.

I'm a candidate for the coroner, a lyric for a song

that I tried to take all in, record it   for an elegy I'd write—one day—

except another black girl was with me

because black girls go missing without so much as a whisper of where.

You are alive, I whisper to myself, *therefore something in you listens.*

Somebody / anybody sing a black girl's song!

Braid secrets in scalps on summer days for my sisters.

Feel my mother's hand on my fire-warm face.

O Shadow Song, whose hill is green and leaving,

I don't know if we're in a garden   or on a crowded avenue   you are here, so am I.

In order of appearance: Morgan Parker, Aracelis Girmay, Patricia Smith, Donika Kelly, Toni Morrison, Sonia Sanchez, Gayl Jones, Audre Lorde, Lucille Clifton, Kiki Petrosino, Lauren Whitehead, Phillis Wheatley, Carmen Giménez Smith, Martín Espada, Nicole Sealey, Tina Chang, T'ai Freedom Ford, Honora Ankong, Phillip B. Williams, John Murrillo, Claire Luchette, Naomi Shihab Nye, June Jordan, Claude McKay, Erika Meitner, Alice Walker, Natasha Oladokun, Ross Gay, Wanda Coleman, Natasha Tretheway, Simone White, Danez Smith, Ilya Kaminsky, Ntozake Shange, Raych Jackson, Chet'la Sebree, Taylor Johnson, Billie Holiday.

LA FEMME NOIRE: A CHOREOPOEM

PRELUDE

In conversation with Ntozake Shange's *For Colored Girls Who Have Considered Suicide / When the Rainbow Is Enuf*, and including questions from Bhanu Kapil's *Vertical Interrogation of Strangers,* a girl—young, Black, perhaps myself—poses a set of questions to my (our) elders and my (our) peers. Somehow, the women are women I (we) already know. Somehow, the women are women I (we've) just met.

WOMEN

Interviewer or Phenix

Fatou Gaye

Salimata

Saffronia

Sweet Thing

Peaches

Aunt Sarah

Pecola

In these characters are the voices of thirty-five women and girls from New York, Massachusetts, and Senegal who range in age from thirteen to eighty-six.

QUESTIONS

Who are you and whom do you love?*

Where did you come from? How did you get here?*

What do you know about ending? About beginning?

What do you remember about blood? How do you remember it?

Tell me about the earth—dirt, the sun, water.

Who is responsible for your skin?

What are your favorite parts of you?

Tell me about a wound or a scar.

And what would you say if you could?*

Who is responsible for the suffering of your mother?*

Tell me about your first love.

Where / what / when do you fear?

How will you begin your family?

What are the consequences of silence?*

Tell me something you've never said to your body.

Who do you remember now?

ON BEAT

At twenty-five, I learn to play the tambourine. I've played it off well, but I am
rhythmically challenged. I have been my whole life. For months, I practiced
catching the holy ghost so as to not misstep, look like an old church mother
when it was my turn to get closer to God. The first time I shouted, my rehearsed
one, two, three, up, one, two, three, up abandoned me like a sprinkle of bodies
alive after a broken down & sinking ship. It's funny the way ghosts get
into your head, your limbs, leave you overstuffed with a praise you don't

quite understand. The same went for the tambourine; I pretend-played
on plates, with my fist against my other hand, on the instrument when no one
was looking or listening. In the Black Baptist church, the tambourine becomes
more than an instrument left for the kid who has no musical talent. The tambourine
becomes a vehicle of spiritual arousal, bounces its *pings* & *pongs* & *dings* off
the body of the player & onto that of those clapping, foot tapping,
& hand waving. The tambourine becomes a Harlem stoop & chat between

girlfriends. The tambourine becomes a catalyst, a volta for every ache you've entered
the sanctuary with that day. At twenty-five, I played an imaginary tambourine
in my mother's living room turned Baptist church. The clang & howl of upbeat gospel
in the background, my mother with the real tambourine in hand, saying *like this,*
like that. I press my palm into the chest of a Styrofoam plate from which I imagine
a *tinging* that mimics my mother's. I am frustrated because I can't seem to get it, I can't
seem to music like my mother, like my

aunts, my great-grandmother, something in my blood is displaced by this knowing.
As I decide on what brand of *different* or *odd* that I am, my mother passes me
the tambourine, her hands as sure as salt-water against sand, & demands that I play.
I hover around the instrument with my mouth ajar like I am hoping to crack a code,
complete an equation, or something. I tap my foot in a rhythm that mimics
the pace of the song playing, & I play. I mean it just like that, I played & I mean it
just like that I had the vehicle in my hand & I moved

it & I mean it just like that my mother & I were on a stoop; chatting & I mean it
just like that my blood was my great-grandmother's again. When I was a child, my
mother, my aunty Brandi, & church-aunt Bertha were the church's
resident tambourine beaters & spirit movers. These three could be found at any part
of the choir stand if a song was in need of a bit more sound that came humming its
beginning through the organ, i.e., my aunt Monte led a song called *Work It Out*,
which is a persona in the voice of God saying, *Stop trying to fix it*

if you say you trust me. Stop interfering if you want me to have my way.
If you really believe that I'll see you through. Move out of my way and let me work it out.
If you can't understand how lyrics like these would incite riots in the black palms
& throats of Black mothers, hood-natives, having seen many a love unjustly in the dirt,
having lived many a check-to-check, having had a host of leeching lying lazy ass lovers &
finally kicked them to the curb, having almost not made it, having almost forfeited their
breaths, then none of

this is for you. If you understand, then you'll understand the circular & wooded
percussion with its metallic zills writhing beneath the drumhead & flash against
the browns of these women. & I typically believe that silver is some less regal cousin
of gold, less worthy of our skin, but something about the coverings of these women
mimicking each stage of blossom made the praise in their pump-gloved-feet, in the waves
of their body-building hips, in their creased & culminated hands (ringed, manicured,
having held a first-born blood at their breasts,

having balled themselves into socks full of pennies over boys, having pushed open
a nightclub door & floated like wind into the church, still a bit red with rum, having
whipped some little versions of themselves leather straps out of fear at the thought that
the little selves could become the same versions of their bigger selves), made the silver of
tambourine limbs look go(l)d against them. At twenty-five, I cannot wait
for my moment where I find the eyes of women, amid a praise I know the name of
& play—beat—music.

SHUG AVERY IDENTIFIES AS PANSEXUAL, POLY, AND DARES YOU TO SAY ANYTHING ABOUT IT

In another life,
I love all things on legs,
all things with wind
and wet in them. In another life,
I tell Miss Celie   God
is everything and she believes
me. In another life,
I am God too. You ever seen a man
big and black like a baobab
fall to his knees 'neath
some body stick   and tar like me?
Ever seen a tongue dewy with spit
begging begging?   No?
Well I told you before
I was God. In another life,
Miss Celie and I lay
in her husband's bed,
a bed her husband lay me down in
the night before and she don't mind.
Don't like the scratch of his stubble
against the silk. I lay
Miss Celie
down, teach her
skin lessons, draw for her
the warmth and volcano inside
her gut with my own mouth
and she believes me.
In another life,
I marry a man, buy a house,
love Miss Celie in it,
love my man in it, sometimes
love a frog-eyed-body who say

I am just a person, not
girl, not boy. In bed,
I lift the scents of
three lovers as new covenant
in remembrance of our makings
here. Come on,
have a whiff.

BE (V.)

To my ex-lovers, I **say**, *I will never marry. I **know*** *I should be alone.*   I **press** my big-boned love
into my elbows and **smash**   them on the dinner table. I **look** into love; it is a glass   I **want**
to **shatter** a chorus of damp limbs against sand-face.   Sometimes, I **capture**

wet bodies with my mouth and **burn**   their bloodied gashed things in my throat-salt. I **know**
I should be alone. I **know**   and **destroy**.   I am a residue   of destructive women—
Shug, Bettie, and Jean. My women   and me have been known   to **ingest**   hot-heavy

selves in between us, a whiskey shot and a lavender god we **raise** from the dead. To **fuck** the men who
ain't even our men, **fuck** them good too, **grin** like split fish when we get home to our men who been
stepping out on us.   To **plonk** on a staired front of a brick building, to **guzzle** Smirnoff

and Pepsi from   our fists, Newport white sticks grinning at our lips.   See,   I am but a piece   of many
a sinful mess: I **broil** my lovers in my belly, spew them like swears   once they have cooled
on my insides.   I, a fragment of fire blackening the things I **abduct**.   In a sea body, I **fuck**

and **fuck** and **fuck** what is mine,   what is not, what has made of me a spine laid out,
I enrapture esophagus   entry in gulps of   trouble and lime with every new somebody
in my bed. I **know** I can't be alone. When I die,   some body will hawk

on my grave,   some other body will hallucinate a ghostly limb   lifting up against their thigh
in memory of me,   the soloist will belt the gospel and all of my women   will **sway**   will **shout,**
sojourn against the dirt   will welcome me.

MOTHER - GOD

BLOOD HOUSE

One time, some almost-body was
there in my cupboard pelvis, got
sucked out of me in the tornado's whirl
and this is not her story. In
the story, I am a house splayed
against a bundle of gray tarp.
I heave a remnant of old loves
into a septic tank, I have no mouth,
in some parts of the light no door
at all. I swell the way water does
flooded hardwood. I smell the way
new flesh does in a river of insides.
I spell a new name in afterbirth,
blood on the welcome mat.

AUBADE WITH BURNING CITY

Is it too forward for me to call my body
the city burning? To say I've arrived here
on many occasions, a molotov cocktail
near-boiled in my fist—my city
two-faced & terrorizing its own people.
My city curvy & loud like I remember
& smelling the way things do after they've died.

Up until this point, I taunted my city
with the possibility of flame, goaded her
with the maybe of cinder. & each time
my city puckered a skyscraper-high mouth
& asked for her cocktail served with lime.
To her, I am but a girl crying fire—
there aren't any villagers in this city
to tire of my howling. This morning,
a pellet of light forced its small will
into the wind-battled curtains. Light came
with a rabid growl & a girl-city saying *burn*
& my city awoke, was hungover
& peeking at what she'd done to herself—
migraine of rubble, thirst of a green garden
yellowed & underwatered. Sometimes,
I am not my city. Sometimes, I watch her
get naked, break shit, build bone to brink
& I don't stop her. Sometimes, I like it.
Sometimes, I am a cocktail mixed
to end her where she stands upright smashing
or where she lies spread & opened.

The fact of the matter is that if my city burns,
so will I. & what does fire know of some creature
like me, like my city, other than its bubble, peel,   & inevitable dying.

HARLEM '94–'04

Monday through Friday is Harlem   after Langston Hughes. A school teacher
asks, *what happens to a dream deferred?* We quick   rising suns and gap-
teeth begging for dictionaries. We stray bullet bodies praying the safe
arrival of dreams despite the skin, the femurs already faded in the cement
of Lenox Avenue. Us girls fall in love with the first woman
since our mamas and argue about whether it is pronounced *An-jill-o*
or *On-ja-loo*, who *laugh like she got gold mines diggin' in her backyard.* We spread
chests and small hips, we think us
women for the first time. *Phenomenal* in peter pan collars and pleated skirts,
milk mouths, and box braids. Saturday night is
101 West 131st Street, my mother smelling of sweetened rum, quick-rolled blunts,
ponytail spritz, and Cool Water perfume. We got bellies full of oodles of noodles and oil-damp
pork chops. Lil Kim reminds the women,   *fuck niggas, get money*   not to worry
about men, cause men   aint worried   about them. The women say
amen, stomp their heels into the floor, squat. Thighs gaping, and tongues hang
from the colored lips. They rap as if Kim be kin or a god. When they leave,
pile into taxi cabs for the club, us girls are in the mirrors—small
thighs gaping and kool-aid tongues hang from our lips, rapping, praying.
Sunday morning is Antioch Baptist Church   and Sarah got a testimony
in her throat, a biscuit and molasses ballad. *Lord do it for me*—then,
riots of black hands wind amongst the stained-glass windows.
*You've read the story about the blind man and one day he heard Jesus
was passing by. He said, lay your hand on me.* The holy spirit is
a wet rash. Here, a collection plate of praise, prophetic patois heavy
feet on blood themed rugs and tomorrow,   we   restart.

ALMOST ODE

*Invitation to praise—
Like a black mother of an unmurdered child
Like a church mother in her flyest Sunday hat
Like the sun-wrapped children in Harlem running into fire hydrate gush*

Up until this point
                the fish bones
                that hold together
                my pelvis have ached.

                And I am no fish
                but easily snapped
                each time you are
                a dream and I am an ocean
                of *if*.

I name your almost   many times   a fuller poem than the last. And I,

black skin and an opening,

                              have been taught to pray to men

                              to believe everything

worth anything is the body   .   that enters

never the entered. And I   have sat in a field of oxalis, empty

of your almost, their grave-plum middles   murmuring

about the everythingness of God according to Shug Avery.*   And thus,

this is a praise song for a god-body,   is a woman*—that I could be

some - thing enough to build a habitat of self*   however brief.

I am a blues tune   for a war*   torn ovarian plain   I am

twenty-one, a wondering   mess, still a milk-   mouth round

my mother's breast   and my mother an oak full of mourning   and her mother

hallowing in the dirt.   And we are a bloodline   of almosts*   and still

praise*   for our holy innards.   And you,   I love like crops

in spring do   the dung-smudged earth.* Praise   the sucking tube flesh that inverts your almost,

petitions the earth for a second chance on my behalf.* Praise   the lazarus tomb in my

gut for my six-week   almost. Praise   the nurse   who looks into the sonogram,

swivels my insides   in the direction of the examination table,   does not compare

your almost to a nut or fruit   of some variety, to hold   when I cannot

fathom my limbs. And I   call you by the almost name   *Kendi Akai Elizabeth Carter**

as if to call you   loved one of a risen sun,   un dead,   un gone,   my girl.*

To say   I—   your almost,   would amass a world   in which you are

a palm   for tracing with my fingers   if given the chance.   To say

that I know God   best because of your perhaps.

TRANCE

INTERVIEWER

Who is responsible for the suffering of your mother?

> *Salimata moves as if she's carrying something, perhaps a baby or something dead*
> *Fatou moves as if she is fighting*
> *Aunt Sarah paces back and forth*
> *Peaches is still*
> *Saffronia trails her face and skin with her fingers*
> *Pecola covers and uncovers her mouth*
> *Sweet Thing tries to conceal her entire body at once*

SAFFRONIA

My mother's mind was fragile, split
open by a baby who wasn't the same color as her.

FATOU

My father   or his second wife
or the oil that she tossed into my mother's welcome.
The familiar *assalamualaikum* before she entered our home
or the pink and peel of my mother's skin from her face.
My mother's eventual crisp or the bloodied tile
of a body she became afterwards. Or my father
and the baby boy he conceived with the second wife
within days of my mother's attack.

> *Women exchange motions*
> *Continue through Aunt Sarah*

AUNT SARAH

I bet my mother was lively. An intrauterine ballet dancer
prancing out the dream of every voice she heard from inside
my grandmother. I often think about the floating, the somersaults,

the anticipation. My mother was a healthy seven pound five ounces,
the womb was where she belonged best
and I believe that my mother's suffering came from
being born.

Women gather—including Phenix, except for Peaches
Peaches stands opposite the gathering

PEACHES

Erasure—

Women are monotone / entranced

ALL WOMEN INCLUDING PEACHES

Black lives matter
stop killing our boys
stop putting our boys in jail.

Every twenty-eight hours   a Black man is killed
by a police officer, security guard, or self-appointed vigilante.
Our boys, our men, our sons, our fathers
our boys, our men, our sons, our fathers.

PEACHES

And me? Who gon come get me? Blood taint
up against me   and it aint no boy's, its mine,
its mine, its mine? And our Black boys, our Cis-
Black boys. I been picking Black boy souls off concrete,
praying their names into every street with all the air I got.
I'm bleeding and I said who gon come get   me?

Gon come get all the Black girls bleeding for Black boy bleeding? Who
gon call my name, pound the asphalt, and *no justice, no peace,* for me?

Peaches is still, she holds herself as if wounded
Women are in trances

WOMEN

Stop killing our boys.

PEACHES

Black Trans woman is beaten to death by a group of men mad
cause they mistook her for a "real" woman.

WOMEN

Stop putting our boys in jail.

PEACHES

Remember the hashtag #EVERY28HOURS?
They saying it was a lie. Say we don't know
death like we do. I don't trust nobody
who investigated that. Cause it feel like it—
like we die every day.

Somebody made it
just about men. And I read it! Every twenty-eight hours
a Black *Person* is killed by a police officer,
security guard, or self-appointed vigilante.

WOMEN

Black lives matter.

PEACHES

Woman said to have committed suicide in police custody,
evidence clamoring like homicide,   nobody charged.
We can't let them forget our girls.
Can't forget us.

Women chant and begin to move as if they are wounded and still entranced

WOMEN

Our boys, our men, our fathers.

PEACHES

A teenage rapper tweets to his ninety thousand followers
the reasons why Black men prefer women of other races to their own.
Say, *y'all bitches talk too much, always angry,*
pussy not pink   enough, got too much ambition,
too much makeup, hair too nappy. Oh, you just Black?

And a little girl gon die cause she refused,
cause despite the tweet, somebody wanted her,
and she don't get the luxury of not wanting them back.

WOMEN

Our boys, our men, our fathers.

PEACHES

Are you listening? Can you hear me?
Can't you see your own blood?

Nobody showed up to a rally for my daughter
who got lead in her abdomen in four different spots cause she fit the profile
of a prostitute. They left her body on the side of the road
on the 47th Avenue Bridge in Birmingham.
Cause there ain't enough girl-
souls unraveled and corpsed
for million man marches and our boys
are always the bigger fish to fry.
Cause our boys are under attack
and yes and yes and yes, I war
for the boys too.

Aunt Sarah is free from trance

33

AUNT SARAH

Too—

Peaches is startled by Aunt Sarah's utterance
then meets her where she stands

AUNT SARAH AND PEACHES

Tamir Rice. Akai Gurley.
Kevin Smith. Mike Brown.
Dontre Hamilton. Eric Garner.
Dante Parker. Ezell Ford.

Pecola is free from trance
She meets Aunt Sarah and Peaches

PECOLA

Too.

Rekia Boyd. Shelly Frey.
Darnisha Harris. Malissa Williams.
Tarika Wilson. Sandra Bland. Aiyana Stanley-Jones.

AUNT SARAH, PEACHES, AND PECOLA

Every day a mourning, every day a blood,
Every day a dying too   and we here
bleeding and dying   too
and ain't nobody coming for Black girls.

Aunt Sarah, Peaches, and Pecola go touch / heal / wake up the rest of the entranced women

ALL WOMEN

Black girl   get gash, gotta give, get
stolen, a rubber sole at her head,
carry baby, carry man, carry body

bags and this picket sign and this fist
don't move, aint never bent for Black boys
and we hurt, leaked
and who

PEACHES

When I go, who gon beat my baby's name into that bridge?

ALL WOMEN

Who gon howl our names? How many Black boys
gon show up
blooded, fist up, and picket sign unbent?

ARS POETICA ON THAT DAY

That day I had come with bags / on my spine / weary / from carry weight / of a most coveted dead thing / that day / I had come / with a ripe and weeping mango in my teeth / that day with love / calling me an almost wife / called the pressing together / of our soft and bursting bodies in bed almost / perfect nearly straight / that day / I had come wanting a séance for my dead / or almost that / at my own hands / or / at the trotters of part-boar-part-cop-creature / or / at the man looking like my brother but not / and yes / looking like my father but not / a deep and quick *fuck you then, bitch* in his fists / and yes / tell me I'm not good enough / that day / I had come / good / and enough with praise /// for muck daughters / worshipped a God that built this earth full / of us / bombs / that day I had come with a split / flesh / in my wrist / picked / up a poem / I bled that day / I had come with Aiyana / Tamir / Akai / Mike / Alton / Freddie / Shelly / Trayvon / Islan / Jordan / Rekia / and / and / and / and / and / and / and / and / and / and / and / and / and and andandandand ransacked the heavy skin in my jaw / I prayed / beat an ancestor scribbled stone / attempted to lazarus them / awaited the spring of their bodies from the dirt/ watched every grave grave still / that day I had come with women / in my bed / one had been staring into me like an angry sun / one asking about my lungs / a mattress wondered me into its body / queried / who are you / and how did you get here that day?

HEAR ME OUT, MY EYEBROW LADY AS

God   is no stranger of mine when I walk
into the threading salon. Rest my feet
upon the swivel chair altar, hook neck nape
into chair's back, lift my eyes to the hills
in her fingers, say my prayer:
just clean them up, not too thin.
& like an *amen*, my eyebrow lady presses
a white & hollow sewing thread onto my forehead.

Hear me out, I feel the same now
as I do in the Baptist church sanctuary,
an altar crowded by burden & shoulders
that sag like thawed ice & the mothers
who seed their knees into temple ground
their mouths spread out like weeds that beg   *God,*
please save my babies, save my marriage, save   me.

Hear me out, I feel the same now
as I do when my pastor douses her copper fists
in oil, signs the cross slick
against the foreheads of us all, & the oil splits
its sacred anatomy
around us like we're water.

& we all know what happens
when water & oil get together—they get apart.
& imagine
the oil is holy & imagine the hands anointing
are holy & imagine the sirens
that must light up the sky

in God's stomach at the holy
substance's sacrifice, at its opening   so that we are born again.

Only in the threading salon, the thread
becomes oil & we are still water. The church ladies
are still the church ladies getting their shit
right,   a prayer   of fresh acrylic,
the rhinestone speckled fists, Dominican salon
blow-outs, & individual eyelashes.
Their seeded knees become a worship
alive in their hands stretching skin under thread.
Only in the threading salon,
my eyebrow lady does the anointing,
signs something equally as holy in aloe vera gel
across my forehead.

My eyebrow lady silent & standing over me,
sharing her testimony, banishing a struggle
of small hairs looking to unibrow, looking
to steal the sun in the birthrighted curve of my brows,
cleaning me up until the next time I need
making   over. Hear me out,
ain't God as good as this?

KALEIDOSCOPE OF GIRL WITH HER TITS OUT

In a dream I am a girl with her tits out.
I am black fins and nipples gyrating against
window glass, and nobody comes to stop me,
to say I can't be what I am very clearly,
here   naked. Black hell fire, an unquenched flesh
looking to feast, until I am fed, until I am freed
and I am   the girl with her tits out.
Clifton is here singing about being here and black,
about breasts, too. *Summertime* and the livin is easy
against the black of my feet. I am Ella Fitzgerald
singing *Summertime*. I am as alive as a pistol
breaking up boy bones on the corner
when it is ninety-five degrees in Harlem.
Summertime, and the boys do not die.
I am a stage—as alive as a pistol, as alive as
a bulletless body in the smoldering hot.
I am Louis Armstrong gargling my flesh
from the devil's hot bed and I am the devil,
hot bed gargling me back—here

                                        It is March,

and Spring hasn't an eye to smell what love
comes out of soot. Soot-love is March on fire,
the petunias melting, and rain-love is wet March.
March is sprinting into almost.

                              See March   run
                              See March   burn.   Run!
                              See love   run. Burn
                              See her.   Run. Burn.
                              See run run
                              See.   see,   see? BURN.

I leave a party with March. I am black fins
and nipples gyrating against window glass. I am out—
the girl out   in a dream. I am just the girl,
chainless and   tits out, singing *Summertime*.

DUPLEX WITH GARDEN

I arrive at an earth and plant myself
cause most gardens instruct their buds away from me

cause most gardens want to kill me
cause I began as a weed spread up into my mother

cause I began as a mother, a weed, spread up into me
cause a mother is a flower flailed upward out the dirt

cause my mother is a flower forged upward out the dirt
young and barely budded   my mother swole

swole and refused a garden's threat to clip me out
we've been a line of women known to clip our weeds sometimes

we've been a line of women known to keep our weeds sometimes
for reasons that are our own; reasons other flowers don't approve of

I reason with my own near-spread weed when some flowers don't forgive me
my weed is rife and merciful   a near-spread altar in my dirt

FAMILY PATHOLOGY

My great-grandmother lights the Newport.
My great-grandmother sits with her fingers as curved as smoke rings,
says nothing, but an occasional *your mother left you*

here with me and being left with her could only mean
un-love. My great-grandmother is a deathbed
and throat-ingesting tumor.

My great-grandmother says nothing
but the occasional *your mother left you*
here with me.

My grandmother is a sun   with her baby in her arms.
My grandmother is twenty-six years old,   hexed,   and rotting   in the dirt,
she is survived by one daughter, nine years old   alive alive.

My grandmother takes with her
the daughter   into the ground, too. My grandmother
is twenty-six years old, hexed,   and rotting in the dirt.

My mother is small-mouthed
and ready-boned beneath a lost boy.
My mother is fifteen years and   an exit

ripping her wrists into starched sheets,
a white coat cups her leaving   in the rubber glove.
My mother is eighteen and alive

without her kinest blood   begging
for the red again. My mother is small-mouthed
and ready-boned beneath a lost boy.

I am born. He is not my father.
I watch my mother   reach   small hands
into the soil when we visit my grandmother's gravesite.

I know nothing of this dirt and cannot help her   dig. I am
ready-boned under a lost boy.   Then,
I am small-mouthed and   an exit, too—

fading in the starched sheet, white coat
cups my leaving in a rubber glove.

PANTOUM IN WHICH I AM A VERSION OF KEISHA
THAT TOMMY KNOWS BETTER THAN TO PLAY WITH

The camera pans to me baby blue-black & glistened in after fuck
I watch my man leave & not for good, the feeling we all want & don't get
The blacklight of television lamp becomes a march of desire ants against my thighs
In the style of my love, in the fashion of his spread fists, the hold of his hunger

I watch my man sleep & not for good, the feeling we all want & don't get
The camera pans to us & reminds itself of the heat, the bodies of us seared in desire
& in the style of my love, in the fashion of his spread fists, the hold of his hunger
I'm a fucking star, you know it. My man knows it, his mouth wet with want

The camera pans to us & reminds itself of the heat, the bodies of us seared in desire
This is the first time in my life   the whole hood thinks   I'm beautiful
I'm a fucking star, you know it. Ya mans & n'em know it, their mouths wet with want
The sky is this bed, this house, love's command, my iridescent little deaths

& this is the first time   the whole world thinks   I'm beautiful
When the phone rings & there is no woman on the other side looking for my man
The sky is this bed, this house, love's command, my iridescent little deaths
The song of myself emptied, black with permanence, & coiled like a quarter moon

& when the phone rings & there are no bullets on the other side looking for my man
The blacklight of television lamp becomes a march of desire ants against my thighs
The song of myself emptied, black with permanence, & coiled like a quarter moon
The camera pans to me baby   blue-black & glistened   in after fuck

ODE TO (MY) PENIS

And you are only mine by proxy, by my being a consensual entryway, by
the calloused fingers of this lover dug into the valley of my spine.   By way of my

humanness, I do have some obsession with owning, place my satchel full of possessive
pronouned things onto an earth-scale each day. Pray this time,   myself   an anatomy

less susceptible to disappearance or to death by way of my blackness and sometimes
perceived lack of ability to have because of it, by way of my queerness and this bed

I've woken in for a month, our fabrics—a direct threat to the existence of men
that exist nowhere but in this moment of poem. You seamstress of sweat-sapped

browns hissing like rain against the dark and ready dirt, the smell of God in love-making.
A lover offers, *look*   *at my dick just sitting there in the bag,* shakes her head perhaps

in small consequence of her perceived carelessness, of you're not being treated like you deserve,
and she is right, you whisper into me like a breeze, make a big-brown wind of me. I want

to say to love something of the beauty in putting a piece of body on, or aside
just for me, make clear something not of my human inclination to possess, but of my

other inclinations toward existing despite the inevitable dangers, the possibility of facing them.
You translator of a language in another abdomen—how you sough it all into my middle,

make me a container full of desire's rounded grin, a deep and quiet *I love you, stay with me,*
other small gnawing things. Administrative assistant to the lover making a spring-fucked

windchime of my larynx, where I ask God if we'll make it to a day where I have—
where I am some part of my lover's hull that cannot be unbuckled after we've come

together and made valleys of our earth's spill into one another.

I DO & WE LIVE

after / for Billie Holiday

If I shake a body down off a death-swole bough
wet with a residuum of lung-wind & song
one of us still gon live & breathe anyway, *hallelujah.*

If I untie the bulge & twist of once-   grin & thick brow,
I'll whisk the black limbs in a silk slip & poke out their hips like prongs.
If I shake my body down off a death-swole bough,

sip from the tit of a gin bottle, get a sorry shit to go down south
& wipe my water clean off his maw, send him tip dry waggin' along,
one of us still gon live & breathe anyway, *hallelujah.*

If I squawk like a deranged ocean with my big black mouth,
Ain't nobody business if I do & ain't nothin but God can get me gone!
If I shake your body down off a death-swole bough

rusted in the blood of our priors & I ask this tree about
the spill—the way we water its green in our livin' songs,
one of us still gon live & breathe anyway, *hallelujah.*

Spread on me like heat when nobody do—can't nobody say how
to save a lady like me off a tree's organ playing a mourning song.
If I shake this body down off a death-swole bough,
one of us   still gon live & breathe anyway, *hallelujah.*

AMERICAN PANTOUM WITH BULLET-HOLES & WALL

The murdered will riot,   rip open their graves
incarnate out the cracks   of street where their
bloods got hard, got stuck rusts   in the cement. The law makes me a grave, |
deadly fires emptied into   me, seeped through my hair.

The streets incarnate | and my cracks shout a name
that is not mine & rightfully so.   I saw the whole thing
a deadening fire barracks its body   into Breonna   's bed | I've seen the taffeta of her slumber,
she never hurt   a thing.

I saw the whole thing, I build   her holed shrine   of myself & rightfully so |
From a dream, she cannot squall at her blood,   her emptying
In a taffeta slumber,   she never heard a thing
I evaporated in bullet circles to wake her & they didn't say her name   til she was not   is.

Her emptying,   her blood,   her squall,   her dream,   her | cannot,
according to kentucky law,   Breonna   had to | was   a justified grave
Breonna is | *Wake up!*   *Breonna* | | BreonnaBreonnaBreonnaBreonna
Murdered! Riot. Rip open your graves.

BLOOD – ROT

SERMON

*"Give not that which is holy unto the dogs, neither cast ye your pearls before
swine, lest they trample them under their feet, and turn again and rend you."*

—Matthew 7:6

Mother god in the name of Girl—I come to you
as alive as I know how asking you to be
an unbloodied knuckle sandwich, be unfucked, and in
an undulant ocean of selves and salt bone of my befores. Be the first word
out of my mother's reborn mouth. Be swine-repellent or the pearls that look
like pearls but don't bust from too much pressing   down. Be that
which is holy and make dogs deathly allergic. Be
me in an un-rendable skin-sheet. Let this poem (Earth? Body?) ? Be all of you
and none of me for the sake of your people.   Amen.

        In this story somebody will say it is your fault.

In the book of Matthew, Jesus gives a speech
to a crowd of people on a mountain. He catalogs the rules
for living a good life. In the present,
an open and calloused fist irons this scripture
into a daughter's mouth—makes pearl about pussy,
squalls into a crowd of only daughters.
Daughters dance like clams out of water, hinge ligaments
torn. Somewhere close by
a factory of pigs awaits pearl in pissy alleyway,
in small budding girl-children, calling them women
as if they don't already have names,
waiting in their classrooms, right here   piggy-zippers ajar,
trotters stroking piggy parts,
and piggy cum. Piggy sound

like a war of dog barks. And anyway
someone will say it is your fault.

In a mucked and shredded glass
the daughter says to her flesh it is my fault—for I came
of a darkened womb, of cement splattered in blood.
Here, daughter becomes a bed saying fault
in every creak of metal spring.
Daughter
becomes fault, becomes mother.
Daughter
birthed into fault. Pigs wait
or don't.

Tell your neighbor—*neighbor, oh neighbor*

we don't all make it out.

Neighbor, oh neighbor

Pecola Breedlove's small body is

a room

of us.

A woman/   on corner/   yells/   my pussy/   my choice./   Listen close/   she has/ a/
murdered girl/   in her throat/   the body/   in tonsil/   reeks of break/   fast meat. The/
woman is/   dead too. This/   corner the/   pearl-less grave/   no cross for/   her headstone.

Every day
when the rapture raises the dead of the earth
some-thing on legs instructs a girl to
know her worth—the instructed bodies
are one pearl, a garbage bag of blood,
no mouth and here. here. here.   Will you come?

CLINIC

doyouhaveanyquestions?wearesendinganantibioticandcontraceptiontothepharmacyonfile.areyoureadytobegintheprocedure?
x, 17 tells friend about anesthesia, says it'll be quick. I will be out of it. I need someone here. friend can't stay.
pee on stick. slick abdomen with gunk. see figure on screen. quick chat. undress from the waist down. drink apple juice.

x, 25 balls her meat into a waiting room chair, bundles flat mouth beneath mess of hair hanging down.
a girl comes for her, girl wraps tongue in the air, asking are you okay. x, 25 just wants to get out of this place.
doyouhaveanyquestions?wearesendinganantibioticandcontraceptiontothepharmacyonfile.areyoureadytobegintheprocedure?

x, 20 is blood. is a tiny heaving set of collar bones, asking her big sister, will it hurt? sister is small sound.
sister knows the story. knows blood and vacant crux. knows it will hurt if she is unsure. knows she can break.
pee on stick. slick abdomen with gunk. see figure on screen. quick chat. undress from the waist down. drink apple juice.

x, 37 has been big with babe four times. the bones clay-thick with tired. stretch marks peek through paper gown.
likely goes home to the children, kisses husband hard on the mouth, says honey I handled it on my lunch break.
doyouhaveanyquestions?wearesendinganantibioticandcontraceptiontothepharmacyonfile.areyoureadytobegintheprocedure?

x, 15 arrives with a boy on her hip. the family, they all sit. she struggles through intake form. kisses the boy's brown.
asks her mother about chronic illness. mother shrugs. she bubbles in no. boy asks what she'll get him on his birthday.
pee on stick. slick abdomen with gunk. see figure on screen. quick chat. undress from the waist down. drink apple juice.

a waiting room in the south bronx is black with x, so many of us they run out of chairs. we run out in brown
paper bags, synopsis of service, prescription. ghosts will call us murderers. judges won't hear our sides of the body. replay,
doyouhaveanyquestions?wearesendinganantibioticandcontraceptiontothepharmacyonfile.areyoureadytobegintheprocedure?
pee on stick. slick abdomen with gunk. see figure on screen. quick chat. undress from the waist down. drink apple juice.

SELF-PORTRAIT AS BLOOD

The snapped tree branch calls my name   knows the swell of my blood   in its sap
and I haven't died yet.   I don't know the trees without my blood   and my bloods too
often become the tree, freshly budded up from the wet   and body-stuffed earth.
And where and where do we go when we die?   Black   and blooded,   before
we tree   before we feed our bodies to dirt?

It isn't as simple as this   our vanishment, the emptying.   Our dead are whole
despite the stones, are vacant of nothing but breath. We know of bloodtrees
of kin become the wind in their leaves. We have prepared for our deaths and it is
as simple as this   our planting, the root. I have watched
the dead in a mirror of country obsessed with a particular hue of dying.

It isn't as simple as this   I want to unearth the bone in this ground
between dead and Black, this limbo between my skin
and the inevitable termination of my breath, my inevitable sprout,
my shallow   my empty   my guts   at gunpoint.

T-H-U-G L-I-F-E

poem should be read bottom to top

but I must defend mine.[1]   (thug, infant, everybody black)   It's all the fuck I got.

Now, I don't wanna hurt nobody,

*homiemother*infant*black* give u hate *back,* give u *graveback. for* the infant *back.*

littlethuginfants*thuggin niggasbrave* u the hate *the grave* u give fucks everybody *the* thug u give every

life */ prison / prison /* cradle*thughategraveprison*fuckeverybody */* littleinfantsthug

/ first toy was gun / black / the cradle / little thug *grave /* get hate *get grave / get*

& penitentiary / thug */ pray with AK /* thug *wishin someone held* thug/infant *but they never did.*

/ one in the chamber ate thug. */* hate give infant *cradle* & *grave.* & *the mothers that cried* & *homies that died*

body life */* thug hate give everybody hate */* everybody   life hate thug */* life ate thug.

infants life */*hate infants */* hate thug */* infants life the hate. *tell me, are you scared of the dark?* hate */* give every

/My first words was, "thug for life!" little infants? */*   everybody? */* body */* hate give little

young niggas be brave. Fuck */* the hate   u give   little infants */* little infants thug thug thug

hate thug */* the hate give life */a young nigga being raised by the streets.*

give hate fuck little infants */* hate fucks */* give fucks */* thug hate   u

& even with this thug livin', will I escape prison? penitentiary chances was an all day thang.

the hate u give   thug */* the little hate */* fucks everybody */* every body hate every   body */

fuck. *do or die, nigga, pull the trigger, don't give a fuck.* thug */* & fuck life.

give hate */* give u the little infants everybody hate */* hate */* hate */

u give   the hate */* little infants give everybody */* everybody

& hate */* give u little infants. */* the u */

to the grave everybody fuck */

from the cradle

---

1 Italics are words / lines borrowed from Tupac's "Cradle to the Grave."

BREAKFAST POEM

Yesterday morning, a white woman walked into a deli on 145th Street in Harlem,
ordered a sandwich—*an egg, bacon, and cheese on a roll.* To the untrained ear,
this might sound typical of a breakfast request, but there are factors

that you must consider. For any listeners that sprout up out
some crack in a sidewalk they knew the name of before they could reach
the bodega counters without the hoist of mama's hip, this order

was an unlawful police raid, was the little boy from downstairs bullet-holed
in the street, was the four-story building I lived in as a child that nobody I know
can afford to live in now. The order in which she requested her sandwich

is a dissertation's abstract for unearthing the genocide in gentrification.
Consider this,   the way you order breakfast in Harlem
is the way of the fast-forwarded cassette tape played at your first block party—

you smash it up on your tongue like a sandwich—call it by all of its names at once
nospacesnobreaths in between. *Baconeggandcheese,* say it with me. The way I ask
for a baconeggandcheese in Harlem is to say, *yo Ock, let me get* a

baconeggandcheeseonatoastedrollwithbuttersaltandpepper. The way to be   of this Harlem
and living   is to know how to order a breakfast sandwich, to know how
to make your mouth the cassette tape fast forwarded or how to make your mouth

the cassette tape spitting up its guts. To know that the bacon comes before the egg,
before the cheese. Forgive me my drama but she brought her narrow tail
into my Harlem—where the deli was mine. The cook was mine. The quarter waters, mine.

The lotto tickets, mine. The dead kids, mine. The breakfast sandwiches, mine. It was
all mine, all black   black buoy   black brewer   black builder   black black

black black   black black   black black   black black. We know the sound
a sizzled bacon body, a scrambled egg wed to cheese slice, how the butter blankets bread
like a congregation of my niggas getting baptized before the new year.

ELEGY WITH BETA FISH

In this tank, I am the entertainment—round water in my mouth.
You *ooh* & *ahh* & *tap tap* from the insides of your hand skin—I *glub glub*
loud as Black grannies *hallelujah* in church service, flap my fins like the wind
against a wooly, greased, & spiraled scalp. In this tank, I am the entertainment.
I swim in & out of holes like girl legs in double dutch cords. I leap
to the crown of my wet home for small pellets like floorboards under jays
at the function. & when I am fed, I burrow my cheeks in a set of rocks
beneath me & you ogle, so impressed by the way I bury my own self,

keep you grounded. The thing about capture & colonization is that at some point
the captured get free, go buck wild, & burn shit down. When I get out
of this tank, wriggle my shimmered & saturated meat from behind this glass,
your world becomes nothing but this tank, I promise. When I get out of this tank,
I'll bring all my homies with me, we'll bring all our wet with us & we'll *tap tap*
& *ooh, ahh, entertain us!* Burrow your cheeks between the rocks of this earth
you've looted, we'll marvel at your neck hanging open like a pussy after birth,
demand you blow bubbles with your blood. Celebrate with flag-like fins,

gills ajar & breathe fine as you get empty, *glub glub* & demand you try & exist
like us. Erupt in glee at your tongue tying its way down your throat, dangle
our murdered cousins overhead—ask if you are hungry & when you rise panting,
gnawing, & nipping at their limp back fins—your ragged chin begging upward,
we'll use the sharp of our mourning to split you like a gill stretched open.
Out of the tank, you are the entertainment, are the pet kept & tapped at.
Now beg for your life—fissured & gutted like me, like my kin
all your red & blue water drained from your gullet.

ALTERNATE NAMES FOR BLOOD:

Altar & Apple pie & Afro & Aniya Germany &
Ambria Baker & Antioch Baptist Church & Aunt
Sarah & Atlantic Ocean & Aiyana Stanley-Jones
& Alima Jones
&
Biiiiiiiiiiittttchhhhh, listen & blunt smoke &
Bitch, you aint that cute anyway & big bones &
Brandi Brown & Brenda Bond & bad touch &
block party & Bettie Jean Harris & Brent, Alabama
& the blackout of 2003 & bellies full & birthing
rooms & boy-crazy girls
&
cutting greens & casket lining & "come celebrate
with me" & church house & courthouse & cackling
on the stoop & cumming & *close your legs like a
lady*
&
Danville, VA & dirt plot & doin Da Butt &
Diamond Crafton & Dorothy Suggs & daddy long
legs & down south & death & dap ups &
Damnnnnnn, ma
&
Elizabeth, as in Shaina Phenix Elizabeth, as in
Bralyn Elizabeth Carmen, as in Jaidyn Alanah
Elizabeth, as in Kendi Akai Elizabeth, as in Bailee
Antonia Elizabeth & eggs scrambled with cheese &
Eugenia Jones & Ericka Monte Etheridge &
everybody Black & end of summer
&
frying chicken & Felicia Jones & *FUCK* & fuck
cancer & Fatiah Lane & folliculitis & Fatou Gaye &
fucking for the fuck of it & FGG, as in friends god
gave, as in fuck'em good girls
&

grits, as in grits with sugar & good touch & God &
gargling salt water & ghetto, as in fabulous, as in
bitch, as in baby mama & gold & grape jelly &
garden & green grapes taste better than red ones
&
Harlem & hot dogs from the stand & hips & hairy
arms & holy spirit & hell & high water & hymns
&
Integra Jones & ivory, not white, wedding dress &
indigestion & inertia & *it ain't over until God says
it's over & iight, I'm on my way*
&
Josephine Coleman & Jimbos Hamburger Palace
& juice, as in baked chicken juice, as in green juice, as
in apple juice & Jameela Simmons & Josette
Tompkins & Jada Jones & jerry curls & Jamaican
spot patties with coco bread
&
Kate Harris & knee scars & kitchen drawers &
kickstands on bikes we never ride & kidney, as in
beans, as in my aunt needed one before she passed
& Krista Jones & Kennedy Fried Chicken
&
The leather belt & Lipton Onion Soup Mix &
limping & luggage & *Lord have mercy jesus* & *Lord,
do it for me* & *Lord, thank you*
&
Motts, as in applesauce, as in my mother's theory
about sex & *Ma, what's for dinner?* & Ma says like
my great-grandmother would say, *hogass & catshit
for gravy* & it means something good & mousse for
fresh box braids & the kids calling my mother
magilla gorilla before she was my mother &
Malcolm X Blvd & Make my Cake & migraine &
meatloaf
&

Nanny Oliver & no headstone money & niggas &
fuck them other niggas cause I'm down for my
niggas & ninety-nine cent store cherry lip gloss &
niggers don't belong here & nappy hair & no good
& Nijah Germany & new growth & Nyrobi Harris
& Nyla Harris & *negative, k*
&
oaths & oatmeal, ocean, Olive Oil Relaxer, Oodles
of Noodles & *ayo, ock let me get a chop cheese on a*
roll
&
all the play cousins & Pecola Breedlove & chunky
peanut butter & piñatas we don't pronounce the
tilde & potato salad & Peaches & pussy, as in
between my legs, as in I *aint pussy, iight pussy, fight*
me then, pussy & pastelitos & piss in the project
elevator & pissy drunk uncles & pens for making
things, for holding babies & Pamela Jones & Palo
Santos burning
&
Quenniqua Martinez & Q-Tips & *Queen Bitch,*
supreme bitch & quarter waters & quotas filled &
quick feet & quick buck & the kids get their
summer thirst quenched by the icee man
&
Roma Jean Brown & Robin White & run & run &
run & riot & rot & revolution & *rest assured* & *you*
look raggedy & remember us
&
Smirnoff with Pepsi & spicy brown mustard & a
dozen snake plants named after one of our deads &
Sweet Thing & summertime shootouts & Salimata
& switch, as in hips, as in tree branch, as in blade &
shirley temple curls with flat twists & spritz &
Shirldina Brown & slaves & Saffronia &
somebody's son & somebody's mama

& somebody's so & so
&
tequila & Tiffany Crafton-Harris & turkey wings
& terminations, as in babies, as in wrongfully from
jobs & Tammy Brown & twerking & tea with
honey & Taste of Seafood
&
Ugly, as in *you ugly, ya mama ugly* & school
uniforms & uppercut & ungrateful kids &
underbelly, as in us, as in Harlem, as in Black
&
Veronique Baker & Velcro Mary Janes & vegetable
oil & venom & Vicks VapoRub & Victoria Jones &
Vanessa Jones & vetted lovers & velour sweatsuits
&
Weave & weed & we & womb & belt welts & *wade
in the water, wade in the water, children* & where do
babies come from? & *why is mommy crying?* &
What is love if it isn't this? & *why, Lord?* & *what
happens in this house stays in this house* & women
who dabble quietly in other women & *I thought he
had a weapon*
&
A xeroxed love letter between tweens &
xenodiagnosis & Xscape & xanthic flower & ex-
lover & ex-con & exclamation mark mouths &
extra duck sauce in the bag, please
&
Yerrrrrrr & Yes & yell & yolk & *yellow is the color
of sun rays* & yams & yesterday & *yessirrrrrrr*
&
off-brand ziploc bags & zipped-lipped kids &
cheap zinfandel & zig-zagged parts & children who
make believe they're zillionaires & *happy birthday
to you, you live in a zoo* & zero dollars in the bank

MOTHAFUCKIN SONNET

Thank you hood rat, hood rat, hoochie mama, you a bad ass mothafucka—
flame for tongue, letting mothafuckas know we tired of wiping

their asses for them. Can I join you on that hilltop? You look like every
thing   God ever made worth something. You—boulder of sun-gold box

braids that soar across your left shoulder blade in neck roll   & acrylics shift
like storm tides in your fist. Thank you,   for letting that nigga Craig know

he wasn't slick even if you *was* wrong. Niggas be always wrong with fists
close as pussyhairtoskin. They wrong, always looking for a country

to get big in, raise their gangly bones from almost graves, yank us down
by the hair. Thank you,   maestro of our three-part harmony of *fuck you mothafucka,*

you think you slick, go on ask that   country for some   saving—the one made
them think girls built in the image of their mamas were for whipping, cause they been

been beat, bullet-holed, buried. Like we too aint been a b & a b & a b & a b—ten-fold(?)
Who is counting?   Thank you, thank you   when we are   a lesser math.

SELF-PORTRAIT WAKING FROM ANESTHESIA

I am something permanent and have no proof of this. And still   And it is
not in the sense that I will live forever, but in the sense that today I wake like
the limbs of fat rats at the hymn of a coming 3 Train. I am not sure
that I won't live forever   when I wake, a poured out water bottle
for a womb, the liquid of who could have been clogging a nearby drain. I want
my mother. I want to mother. *Don't let me die,* I beg. I pray for something
meatier than salvation. Something like water. I am permanent in the way
that my lungs are no end-stopped lines. My breath is a long poem. The night
before surgery, I drink water after the recommended cut-off time. I blow
a bubble in the water, a whisper into the bottle cap. I hoped I might do what
the doctors said I could—choke on my tongue, die a mouthful of letters or
conceive again or adopt or become diabetic if I keep going the way I'm going
or kill myself. I count backwards from ten. I never make it to one. I never
make it.

REVERSE GHAZAL IN HARLEM

For the sake of this poem, I'll call you my nigga—
my play-cousin from downstairs; a girl I played house with; the nigga

I loved like the projects do the sound of Mister Softee's truck. Walk and talk with me, nigga.
Come on. I ain't got all day. The three train is delayed and it's as hot as satan in a coat.

These white folk got comfy, pasted in yellow-brown seats past 96th Street. What is this shit my nigga?
You remember a few years back, train cars got hollow and black as tooth-cavities at each street number's rise?

They put a bistro at the root of 101 West 131st; an amalgamation of brick that held me—kept a lot of my niggas
out of trouble, out of wet dirt, out of cells, out of symbiotic inclination of niggas to dying. They like their steaks

like they like us. Runny—running—rivering plasma onto their tables (coroner's or dinner.) Harlem niggas
glare at police cranes; don't walk up to new neighbors saying, *go back where you came from* to survive.

Remember us: We pronounced 125th as *two-fif*. We high school sophomores in H&M acting like niggas.
We in pleated skirts, grinning like open zippers at the boys in polo t-shirts and uniform slacks.

In the bodega—ordering a *baconeggandcheese* on a toasted roll.   Whatchu want, my nigga?
My teenage father posed in this very store between potato chip racks and quarter water coolers.

Remember me: a pendulum of butt-length box braid ignoring the hiss of corner niggas,
Awa curled her inky fingers around kanekalon, lathered my scalp in Soft-Sheen jam.

My mother spit me out of her nine-month brew. In Apt. 8, speakers humming, *fuck niggas get money*. In Harlem, before I learned I had a mouth I mimicked music on the pavement.

Finish this lyric as a nigga preservation spell: *Hey ma, what's up, lets slide, alright* _____
My mother asks, *Shaina, how does it go? We fly high, no lie, you know this* _____

FAMILY PATHOLOGY WITH ALTERNATE UNIVERSE

My great-grandmother unlights the Newport.

My great-grandmother says *I love you.* The mattresses

of her palms carry the bodies
in my jaw. My great-grandmother plants

a seed meant

for eminent sprout. My great-grandmother is

un-smoke, un-throat   ingesting

tumor, un-in the wet   earth. My great-grandmother
says *I*
love you.

My grandmother lives.

My grandmother boils bone

into two babies, perhaps Jada and Joe

or Reggie after her brothers. Or

Bradford Jr after her lover.

My grandmother's blood
runs
like a wild and crazy weed in her daughter's flesh

so she never leaves her dirt at home.   My grandmother lives.

My mother

siren mouthed and hair

around her scalp like a fire,

says, *my mother is at work*

if you want to come over. She is sixteen

and getting caught

sneaking my father into the turtle-green bedroom. My mother says *don't*

have the abortion. I am born, maybe

when she is sixteen and he is my father.

My mother is kept

in the body, in bed-arms,
in the mouths of all her kin.

My mother says   *don't*

have the abortion. I never

leave my dirt at home

because my mother never leaves hers.

I have

a small breath born of my blood. Say to the breath,

I love you. I

am wandering

albatross atman

with my breath,

plumage of lovers,

of loving, of loves and been loved.

                                                    I bathe

my small air in seeds

meant for eminent sprout. Plasma is wild

in the skin.   I have

                              a small breath
                                                    born
                                          of my blood.

WHY I BE TRYNA LIVE HOW I BE TRYNA LIVE

Cause my niggas stay

        dying   & I know a pattern when I see one.   I know a nigga when I see one.

& I know how to end like the Lord's Prayer   —   cause blood is *our father who art* & heaven

is a stolen museum painting   I stand before mimicking the crooked neck &

hope-choked babbling of a mother   having watched her child die.   Cause I am a mother,

anesthetized & unable to stop my child from dying.   I got something to live for & I call her Kendi,

sometimes real low just so people ask me   to repeat myself, just so I can say her name,

again & I hear God   in the hackberry tree outside my window   whistling like a cat-caller

with a little home training.   Cause I've been called dead & *sista-*   *girl* &   a great

fuck & selfish & a waste   & just like my mother   & a black bitch   & you get it,

but least I still got a name.   & I aint no punk ass bitch either & I know time

got beef with my black ass—wanna run down on me in the street,   stomp me out

with the rubber fist of its Timbos.   Cause I know I own nothing.

Cause I know every time that I've looked to my body *mine*-mouthed,   a God giggles—my(?)

pussy cackles like a stoop of gossips,   I mean it,   my skin snickers black & beaten to a pulp, *look*

at the world.   I know I own nothing   & some man or other manifestation of the earth's tantrum   gon come to collect me   dressed   in his

best   legislation,   best way to call dead things dead & make anybody believe it

& what I look like   just going with them? I got something   to live for   my daily bread,

a borrowed bone on earth   as it will be in heaven   I hope, my hallowed names,

trespass against me   before I am ground   or a body returned

to whoever it really belongs to   & I'll beat your ass.

KIN – ALIVE

TO BE NAMED SOMETHING ELSE

"Every name is a name for God."

—Melissa Febos

when I walk up to the altar to drop my palm-wet & crumpled offering into the basket,
when my dress is just slightly above my knees & it is summer & I am not wearing stockings
& I do not carry a prayer cloth, the church mothers call me over, & not by the name
my mother ordained me after birth. They chorus me, *something else* & I'm as good as gold
or God or gall or girl or gush or get. Something else to mean something alive—here—
holy to mean my not knee-length dress, my bare & buttered calves glittering. I am all name
—a body of names. I call myself   satisfied supine spent   something else. I know
myself, blood of something, blood of else, blood of things. I overhear
two-year-old Bailee singing to herself in the bathroom mirror & thanking the auditorium
full of imaginary everybodies & she pauses as if to accept their love, to appease
their collective beg for an encore, for her to be again a mouth of honey & pop rocks.
Around the corner, I find myself thinking, that girl is something else. Find myself
thinking that girl is a little mouth of God. That girl is   That girl is
& to be named something else is to be named   anyway.

SONNET WHILE BLACK

things happen when tequila, black girls, pressed
glitter & tina snow get together.

a gospel of real hot girl shit, we blessed
& doused in sweet water, mouth bones unfettered.

early on, we chant at the top of our bronchial trees
neva let a broke nigga sex me, neva been scared of the money.

we   a venue of sparkling selves caroling this creed
backsides bob atop plush seats, fleshes unraveled like honey.

after, we still dance, sing, drunk, & cackling
like our mothers do on our childhood stoops.

even after there are two policemen at the front door,
& three squad cars outside asking to come in, take a look,

the house is a sanctuary of us, we are in the spirit, for
we such holy selves, we escape the night, our bodies un-took.

DENIM ODE

Cause you were the bad bitch's first catalyst, the '90s hottie,
skin oiled & tossed in the heat of a Harlem's summer sun.

You made the girls into gods who ruled over the tore up sidewalks,
the ambidextrous stoops, the men panting like dehydrated dogs.

You painted your waters onto skin & became it—light,
indigo, acid, mid, stone, rinse, black, vintage, wash(ed)

the streets clean of the sin of summertime wars
& the 69 Boyz bellowed, *I want you to look*

at them girls with the daisy dukes on! & how
could anyone with eyes not look, see round-ass-spread into you.

& they called it peach, applebum, bubble butt, *Bonita Bonita Bonita*,
& *Tanya got a big ole butt (oh yeah)* & an ass called

by any fruit name, any   thing with juice—an ass incanted like a psalm
is indeed an ass—certified booty, especially

if it can be seen spheric, spread out like a legion,
& rivering amongst a strut in tight jeans.

My god, you kept the hood together—uniformed us
in your armor-reminiscent heavies, made oceanic mosaics

of our people, made black to double as the color of water
& the irony was not lost on us, for our bodies became

the blood-wet cemetery of our once forced dead.
& denim, more Black people get held in you

than they do in a church house & I mean that with God
& with love & I mean that

checking my reflection   & telling my best friend,   girl, I think my butt getting big.

OPENING

Women are sitting in clusters of chairs
Chairs are enclosed in a drawn chalk box on the ground
Each woman has something to leave, break, or take off by the end
The interviewer has a chair apart from the women

INTERVIEWER
I am only here
for answers to a few questions
about your being and the ways
that you are still becoming between the abundance
of land whose people try to erase you—
will you bring me to the spaces
that you have found for your body
to exist inside of
femme noire, mother, sister, friend
tell me of an existence,
for me, for the other young
and girls growing—prepare us
for what could be, protect us
from what should not.

May I begin?

Women nod

Who are you and whom do you love?

Fatou walks from chair to front
There is a spotlight front stage on Fatou

FATOU
Ancestor Lucille Clifton
wrote it, plain as white flour,

"come celebrate
with me that everyday
something has tried to kill me
and has failed."

Come on now, don't be shy.

A celebration with dancing / laughter / a song—Golden by Jill Scott

- -.

An interruption (a thump, a scream?)
Women freeze, stage is dark
Spotlight to Peaches and Aunt Sarah

PEACHES

How many times have I been here? Black and woman
I'm standing right here

AUNT SARAH

foot sole saddling asphalt.
How many times
on a corner, waiting? I love you

Stage is dark, all women form a line

- -

Light on women

SWEET THING

a poem, a pussy
a breaking open of myself
a war   backhand landing, sunflower

ALL WOMEN

the broke back, the hold that
and that and that and that and that, and *bag lady*
you gon hurt your back, walk   now, go down,
get up, get fucked,   shot down, my body
my body, my body   she gone. Been long. We here,
been here.

Dark

– –

Women are in their chairs
There is light

AUNT SARAH

You can call me Aunt Sarah, baby, and I am weary-
boned, been cyclically misused, but let a motha try
and knock me down, now, any motha out there.
I am peering   from the third-floor window
in Lincoln projects, the children
are spilling from the doors of P.S. 197.
I will love until I don't,
simple as that.

FATOU

Fatou Gaye and I am
of the Bedick people, nestled
at the base of a mountain
drought flushed our ancestors from moons ago

SAFFRONIA

I am half, a cross carried
between nappy and a palatable wave. Between

El Barrio and Jamaica Avenue,
arroz con gandules and collard greens
with neck bones.
Between Black? Called Saffronia.

SALIMATA

Je suis Salimata. I was birthed in the mouth of Dakar.
J'aime le soleil ou la liberté.
Ils sont les mêmes, pour moi.

PEACHES

I am of war,   a seedling spared of genocide
budding in avengement.   I am of my mother
who bore twelve children—myself, six like me, and five not.
I love my people, that's it. I'm Peaches, by the way.

SWEET THING

They call me Sweet Thing and I was named for the kind of avalanche
that I can birth up out a body after I wrap it up in me.
And you're looking for your own disaster,
I'll be on the M7 line to 141st Street
or in the LES around the corner from Katz's Deli.
I love long legs, bold arms, and chests atop my own. Always.

PECOLA

I'm Pecola
you ever heard of that hand game?
How does it go again?

Pecola is pregnant
She struggles up from her chair
Prepares to play the hand game with the air in front of her

Mailman mailman do your duty
Here comes the lady with the big fat booty
She can do the pom-pom she can do the twist
Most of all
She can kiss kiss kiss
K-I-S-S.
Ever ran through it so many times
that you almost end up in a split
knowing you can't do no split?

PORTRAIT OF MY MOTHER BEFORE SHE IS MINE

Somebody set the dinner table / a table / no one eats at / & not
in the way of a table set & a fridge-empty / but in the way of
my mother / before she is my mother / never alone in her own
house / maybe the door is unlocked / or everyone has a spare
key / everyone brings the girl or guy over they can't bring home
/ they sprawl / into each other's bodies on the futon / they
wake / before my mother, before she leaves / for work / poke
at the sleeping date's arm to say, *you gotta go before my big sister
wakes up, / it was fun. /* My mother is everyone's big sister. Set
the table / a table / no one eats at because there are too many /
glistened-soil-selves scattered about / coiled into their living /
partied into her living room / at the table you will find / rum in
the kitchen cups / dutches gutted like whitings at the fish
market / too many brown-hued lip pencils, their points dull
from the assortment of mouths thick with Lil Kim lyrics / set
the dinner table / that is actually the blunt rolling station /
that is actually a bar / that is actually a vanity / that is actually
my mother's first child.

Get the Moët, there's got to be Moët. Don't you shake that
bottle before you pop it, niggas aint got money to waste.

This my mama house & she don't know she my mama yet.
Unless, this is a balcony on Virginia Beach

& the Moët, the niggas, the money in question don't belong to
my mother & she & my play aunties met some niggas

at the Norfolk State dormitory & the niggas pulled up for
homecoming or something like that & don't all go there

flashed dollar bills & shiny car rims, at my mother, at her girls
& the niggas thinking they dupped some young dumb girls

into coming with them to Virginia Beach, to a hotel & not
knowing that my mother, her girls, peeped them

from the window, they checked their reflections in the lobby
glass, pushed their breasts up into their chins, pulled their belts

tighter to accentuate their already small waists & round asses.
Unless, before my mother is my mother, there's a car of them,

glowed with the guts of summer desire pasted on to their skins,
undressing towards the beach. If   /   then, shake the bottle

before you pop it, drip it on the heads of passersby below,
somebody got money to waste. This is a music video.

My mother, the vixen. The love interest. The one who wakes in
the morning & cooks pancakes for everyone using a fork to flip.

THE APOCALYPSE COMES FOR US

Harriet parts the sea like a scalp before cornrow. An owl with a boombox face   clicks a cassette tape beak—squawks, *Cash money records taking over for the 99s and the 2000s.* We   ass avalanches   falling down thigh mountains. State—country—land   borders become porch screen doors. A Black girl in Puerto Rico slaps together her palms in celebration of our shared bounce—I, *yasss bitch* at her; she,   *dale mami* at me. We twerk mid-air,   a current of backsides float. Foot soles rise and plant themselves in the wind, gliding toward the gaped salt. We are instructed by the collective, imagined voice of Madam CJ Walker   to   go grab the hair bin. We coo at the barret, bow, bead, and bo-bo stuffed plastics like we do at black babes just home from birthing. We *ooh* and *ahh* at the accessories of our childhoods rained amongst us. Madam CJ sings a long song   it slides   across our skins like hot combs   hovered   around the kitchens at the backs of our necks and we pray we don't get burned.   Madam CJ's song is   like somebody's mama done caught us doing something we had no business doing and she's on the phone right now with our mama who's waiting for us   at the apartment door with her belt   or a look hurt   worse than whoopins.

//

A budding girl-body materializes overhead, asks us to call her everything but dead, fashions her lanky limbs into a ship at the water's mouth   *HMS Aiyana Mo'Nay Stanley-Jones* scribbled on the ship's hip. Little sun-soaked girls meet us on the deck, all fros and spirals swishing around their heads like fall leaves in a quick breeze. On deck, Juvenile fades out like the last song at the function—the one before the lights come on—Madam CJ straightens the fur of her voice into silence. Every little girl on board hopscotch jumps towards a bigger girl—plants their bottoms on the wood. We follow. We fasten ourselves behind their small bodies, hair bins open like doors, we jam, gel,   grease, twist, braid   say—*girl, sit still 'fore you mess up my parts.*

//

And we go down, Moses holding open water portals, sail to Black heaven in lemonade braid, tight-twist-out, greased scalps, 99 cent lip gloss tubes for each of us. The little girls, all glittered and asking—*What becomes of us all   after this?*

GHAZAL FOR BLACK GIRLS IN MIAMI

In the salon, foot soles bathe, black fingers fondle through neon gel colors, green alive.
Hard brush swoops, Göt2b glue wades in fivehead waves, and baby hairs cover, sea alive.

Thee Stallion is water through speaker faucet, waists whine, hot boys hover, greed alive.
Syrup backsides, twerkologist minds, tequila treasures, hype their sisters, she alive.

Fat Tuesday big cup in palm grove, margarita mouths, drunken limbs flutter, leave alive.
Makeup brushes sweep hotel room wind, the skirt, chunk heel, gold shadow, summer, free alive.

Biker shorts leaf the thighs, nipple rings grow through fitted crops, skin bark butter, tree alive.
Beach bright with bodies, hungry clicks of iphone cameras, *yasss bih* wonder, see alive.

Paint the bones in bodycon, decide on gloss, selfie note for the lover, gleam alive.
Lay in the sun, say *black girls don't need screen*, the skin unravels like thunder, heat alive.

Roll insides of plant to paper, merlot lip stain at its tip, blunt mothers, weed alive.
Three am pizza, henny at ten, lemon pepper wings for the culture, eat alive.

We stuff small bags with cloth body, cathedral this living we have conjured, speak alive.
On South Beach, I, poet, Black girl un-break, squad of Gods come of Black mothers, we alive.

BAD BITCH NATIONAL ANTHEM

> *"If you say a bitch, say she that bitch.*
> *If you say a bitch, say a bad bitch."*
>
> —Young MA

lift every voice and sing

    one time for the birthday bitch

til earth and heaven ring

    two times for the birthday bitch

ring with the harmonies of liberty

    fuck it up if it's your birthday, bitch.

let our rejoicing rise, high

    as my best friend after

    her fifth blunt of the day,   high

    as the shot glasses raised for the first time

    in years, all of you and your girls

    together in one place,   high

    as the dollar amount for the 36-

    inch lace front that we can't tell is a lace front,

    for its install in the living room

    of a self-made beautician / nursing

    student / mother of one.

let it resound loud

    as the prayer circle of bitches speaking in

tongues around a twerk, a sturdy milly rock,

loud   as us drunk and belting sad girl

songs like we wrote them, when niggas aint shit,

when we hurting, gone as Monica.

sing a song full

> of the Telfars, the tats, the tiger-striped

> asses, the tellys we fucked in.

sing a song full

> of the tips on our fingers, the tabs we aint

pick up, the talcum on thighs, the tabernacles we

praised in, the tangles in our hair before wash day,

the tabletops we danced   on.

facing the rising sun of our new

> apartments, hairdos, bodies, lovers,

days   we still living.

let us march on

til we glittered in bad bitchery

in every   dancery.

NANNA SAYS, LORD HAVE MERCY JESUS

a nested arroyo

and the world is not on fire
or maybe the world is on fire
and her proclamation is water is
extinguisher is   . The world
is a dining room, boiled and served black—
Nanna watches her loves swallow a dinner
whole, a dinner prepared with her hands.
All her blood and not blood,
their identical grease grins and spice-soaked
fingers cleaned by licking. Nanna says,

> *lord have mercy jesus* on the phone in the dining room,
> wearing my favorite pink and blue pajama pants set,
> concrete-grey laces of straight hair decorating her chest,
> and it sounds like one long and excited word. As if
> there is a God more God than the one that fathers Jesus,
> as if they got their names from this God. As if she is the only
> one to know God, for real, and her only church is the table.
> Nanna watches my little sister in a dance competition on Facebook,

exclaims, *lord have mercy jesus, that girl is long as pregnancy*
moves like a flag in a summer breeze, that girl is something
else. And to be named *something else* is to be named
alive and possible—fulfilled ancestral aspiration. My Nanna is
something else. She is alive and possible, is her mother Kate Harris's
fulfilled aspiration. Perhaps, Nanna's special God calls her something else, too,

> or better. Nanna calls, *lord have mercy jesus,*
> *I was like a plane with one wing,* and I
> imagine my grandmother, a one-winged plane
> trading secrets with her God, alive as rain.

HOW WE HEAL WHEN WE DIE

In conversation with Physiology. Class in emergency work.
From Hampton Album *(1899–1900) by Frances*
Benjamin Johnston.

In the schoolroom healing spot, between   Clifton
Blvd and Madam CJ's Street—the women

séance the cicatrix, sage out disease, swaddle the newborn black things
in Dax hair grease   life everything   that is dead somewhere.

*

Audre calls, *Aiyana Jones.* Harriet carries
a palm-tree girl of fifteen, a bush
of unwinding tendrils overhead,
arms dangly as old skin, legs running
like cut open dams.   *What you done broke now, girl?*

Miss Harriet, it was the last quarter, Aiyana builds her fist
into a measuring stick—*I was this close*
to the hoop, game point,   *Rekia Boyd passed*
the ball and I had to lay it up.

And you come down like a flood?   Aiyana nods. Harriet wraps,
kisses the girl on the forehead,   *Keep coming down, ya hear me? It let you know you alive.*

*

Audre calls, *Mary Turner.*

Mary is eight-months swole with three babies, say
she want four more, waddles
to the table, waits.

OB Hennie Lacks,   or Henrietta (for long),
corks her fist in a rubber glove, waters
the slicked palm against the bulbous black.

Mary massages a soft tune into her abdomen,
tiny folks underneath her ribcage dance
and dance inside. Hennie joins in,
humming Ella's *A-tisket, A-tasket.*   *   Soon, a room of them throb with song.
                                                         Soon, a room of them are alive
                                                         and well.

HYMN

build your hopes on things eternal, and just hold on to God's unchanging hand

build: origin / in the beginning God / hold / plant a seed / be / dance
your: body / possessions / borrowed things / on / specific bone / stolen things they still belong to
hopes: gregarious want / stopped sop of blood / kin / to / not kin / the children / what you can't say
on: the inside / in / under / gods / within / because of / the subject / atlantic / at the top of
things: everywhere / unchanging / here now / boat / oakwood / cedar / bullet / dead now / now
eternal: body of salt / hand / light / a light / niggas / dark / dark / body of / water / spill / heart

hold: keep / bring to a halt / preserve / raise / raise / build / fight / in a fist / in the mouth
on: in this position / for / to cover / to protect / your / séance / illuminate / speak in tongues
to: arrive / edify / cessate displacement / home / replace / hopes / survive / your
god's: sun / rhythm of this current / on / starshine / grave / life / crocus of magic
unchanging: same / eternal / black skin / black / skin / things / spelling of your name / the consistent
hand: ocean that eats / feed ocean / eternal / ocean that be / ocean that free / ocean / ocean /
    perpetual salt

—

1. In the beginning, God borrowed things   stopped the sop of blood on the inside
    of everywhere a body   of salt to keep, to cover,   to cessate displacement.
    Rhythm   of this current,   same—an ocean that eats.

2. Plant a seed of possessions,   of gregarious wants in oakwood,   a light to
    preserve in this position survives the grave, the spelling of your name,   an ocean that be.

3. Dance your body   into what   you can't say   at the top   of now
    dark in a fist. Séance,   edify God's black skin   ocean.

4. Hold on   to God   's unchanging   hand
    build   your   hopes on things   eternal.

5. Be.   Stolen things they still be-lo-on-ong   to the children under boat,
    cedar, bullet, body of spill. Protects   the arrival of sun,   of black, of perpetual salt.

6. Origin of specific   bone of kin   and not kin   the subject here now niggas
    fight   for your life   your black things—this ocean   that free.

GENESIS

1 In the beginning God made from nothing the heavens and the earth. 2 The earth was an empty waste and darkness was over the deep waters. And the Spirit of God was moving over the top of the waters. 3 Then God said, "Let there be light," and there was light. 4 God saw that the light was good. God divided the light from the darkness. 5 Then God called the light day, and called the darkness night. There was evening and there was morning, one day. 9 Then God said, "Let the waters under the heavens be gathered into one place. Let the dry land be seen." And it was so. 10 Then God called the dry land Earth. Called the gathering of the waters Seas. And God saw that it was good.[1]

11 Night and big oak sway in the wet dark for a land losing the bloods of their mothers. 12 A séance of black plum, bisque brun, dirt gold, aphotic rose, they catapult their bodies—sink in chain metal. 13 Babies beg to swim from bodies. Carry the mother left, praying in beach flesh for the child, the sister, the husband—back. Carry the boy bones thrown into the cold mouth when it was day. When he got too sick. Carry girl, hanging from the father's bicep like bissap from the vine. 14 Morning rises with the tired bodies bruised by snatch, from white hole swallows the homes, the peoples, living and not living. 15 Piranhas ingest metal from wrists and ankles, leave the souls with welcome. Algae rise like angry waves, wrap the gashed limbs, pudenda, and the bush hairs. Withered weeds, fin *welcome*. Megalodon sharks shiver their fins onto the black spine cords, say spine to the spine, say breathe to gill draped in spine bone too. Shining big tooths say *welcome*. Slick rocks rub themselves in anemone, spread the stone ligaments into psychedelic olio of home—in hut, in palace, in structures that point their fingers through sunlit cerulean. 16 A city of color welcomes them home.

17 God-mothers get ordained by sunfish. The metallic meat sways in the bit of light on water. Bring the mothers, sunfish say *eat of me—the silvery flesh, that you carry the light of earth in this sea, the priestly parasite, that it may feed the pleated hands with all of its magic, swallow the tough bones, that they anchor the flesh in your people.* 18 Sunfish souls guide mothers to their people. 19 People: a compilation of tongues, spectrum of sunskins, watching the children breathe salt bubbles through their backs. 20 God-mothers swim above them, the people, the city. 21 Sing—*live, live, all my people live. Breathe, breathe, all my people breathe. Free, free, all my people free.* 22 Amen.

---

1 Gen. 1:1–10

NOTES

In "Lucille," the phrase "starshine and clay" comes from Lucille Clifton's "won't you celebrate with me."

Moments of language in "Nong" come from Nina Simone's "To Be Young, Gifted, and Black."

"Aubade with Burning City" is after Ocean Vuong.

"Harlem '94–'04," uses a line from Maya Angelou's "Still I Rise."

"Ode to (My) Penis" borrows its title from Destiny O. Birdsong's poem.

"T-H-U-G L-I-F-E" is using both ideas and language from an interview with Tupac Shakur in which he explained that "THUG LIFE" is an acronym for "the hate you give little infants fucks everybody."

The italicized words in "Bad Bitch National Anthem" are lyrics from "Lift Every Voice and Sing."

"Nanna Says, Lord Have Mercy Jesus" is a nested arroyo, a form created by poet Noelle de la Paz. The nested arroyo is comprised of at least three stanzas that contain an even number of lines. Every stanza has two fewer lines than the stanza before it, and the last stanza contains four lines. The middle two lines of each stanza (or close variations of those lines) become the first and last lines of the next stanza. You can think of it as prying a stanza open to expand it into the next stanza. The two middle lines of the last stanza are the first and last lines of the first stanza, which closes the loop.

"Hymn" sings along with and is working to imagine the other languages in the hymn "Hold to God's Unchanging Hand."

ACKNOWLEDGMENTS

Thank you—

to every eye, every mouth, every hand, every clap, every dance, every every that lent itself to the life of this book. Thank you, God / spirit / body / all my babies / all my loves / all my dead / all my people***

To the following publications for previously publishing several of these poems: *Crooked Arrow* ("Ghazal for Black Girls in Miami" and "Family Pathology with Alternate Universe"); *Dialogist* ("Sermon"); *Frontier Poetry* ("Hydrant Ode"); *Glass* ("Elegy with Beta Fish"); *Puerto del Sol* ("Reverse Ghazal in Harlem"); *Salt Hill Journal* ("Family Pathology"); *Shenandoah* ("I Do & We Live"); and *West Branch* ("Kaleidoscope of Girl with Her Tits Out" and "Clinic").

To the University of Arkansas Press & Patricia Smith for giving these poems a home together.

To Honora & Bessie for every emergency editing session, for every poorly chosen alcoholic beverage, for every pump up, for every laying on of hands, for every bit of love y'all poured into me and my poems. I am forever in your debt, you both forever in every poem.

To my poetry-godmother, Aracelis Girmay—for everything I'd need an entire other book to list. But thanking you now for introducing me to my own possibility, to the sound of my voice, to Lucille Clifton, to to to & on & on . . .

To Erika Meitner, for holding & combing through the very first iteration of what became this manuscript.

To every teacher, mentor, and guide—Natalie Sowell, Carmen Giménez Smith, Matthew Vollmer, John Murillo, Lucinda Roy, R. A. Villanueva, Frances Greathead, Tina Chang, Terry Gadson.

To the ones who saw & knew—Toni, Sarah, Kameesha, Robyn, Lauren, Sky, JT, Aura, KJ.

To Antioch Baptist Church for teaching me something about this gift, for letting me decide how I intended to use it.

To the old Harlem.

To the OG *La Femme Noire* cast. These poems wouldn't exist without first your cackles & movement & work & trust in me.

To my love, because you are here now & I hope forever.